70/1662L

Gospel Hymns We Love

Your favorite composers
share a few of their favorites

Piano Settings by:

Pepper Choplin

Mark Hayes

Lloyd Larson

Mary McDonald

Ruth Elaine Schram

Larry Shackley

Editor: Larry Pugh
Music Engraving: Linda Taylor
Cover Design: Jeff Richards

ISBN: 978-1-4291-0091-5

Lorenz
www.lorenz.com

From the editor...

We proudly present the third in a very successful series for piano featuring creative settings of hymn favorites from six of your favorite composers, this time focusing on *Gospel Hymns We Love*.

As before, each composer chose two favorite hymns and wrote a few paragraphs about why these particular gospel hymns are special to them. Most hearken back to a childhood memory or a particularly meaningful event in their lives. In some instances, the memory shaped the new arrangement. One can easily envision the Grand Tetons in Pepper Choplin's Copland-esque *Solid Rock*; the ringing of the carillon is clearly captured in Larry Shackley's *He Leadeth Me*; the flowing water depicted in Lloyd Larson's *Like a River Glorious* reminds us of God's constant presence and perfect peace; Mary McDonald's stylistically pleasing homage to the founder of the company she has been with since 1991, with E. S. Lorenz's most famous hymn, *Tell It To Jesus*; the child-like joy expressed by Ruth E. Schram in her lilting rendition of *I Know Whom I Have Believed*; or the fusion of gospel and jazz influences on Mark Hayes with *Standing on the Promises*.

The stories are both enlightening and telling of the life-long faith of each composer. The musical settings are equally remarkable in their freshness, stylistic variety, and compositional talent displayed within each hymn arrangement. And, once again, it has been my privilege and joy to serve as editor for such an incredible group of people whose talents are exceeded only by their Christian commitment as they live their daily lives. No doubt these heart-felt settings of gospel favorites will evoke memories of your own musical and faith journey as you play them and, I believe just as surely, as your listeners hear them being played.

—Larry Pugh

Contents

Level Descriptions

Level 1: Easy to moderately easy rhythmically and in technical demands; hands mostly in the middle of the keyboard

Level 2: Intermediate to moderate difficulty with a variety of musical styles; expanded range and more rhythmically demanding

Level 3: Advanced musically and in technical demands; use of full keyboard, scale and arpeggio passages, and stylistically demanding

4

Thoughts from Lloyd...

Like a River Glorious

Being a resident in the land of 10,000 lakes (Minnesota), water is pretty central to our entire culture. We play *in* it in the summer and *on* it in the winter. It is a huge part of our economic base throughout the year. But for all of us, water is central to life. Without it, we do not last very long. I am impressed by the frequency of water references in the Bible. The children of Old Testament Israel miraculously crossed water at the beginning and ending of their 40-year journey to the promised land. Jesus was baptized by water as He began His earthly ministry. He even called Himself the source of "living water." In Revelation, the heavenly New Jerusalem is described as having a crystal-clear river flowing from the throne of God and down through the middle of the city.

This wonderful hymn of promise reminds us that, like the centrality of water to our life and faith, so is the promise of God's presence and perfect peace. As we acknowledge and place our trust in the promises of an eternal and loving God, our faith grows and is consistently renewed from this boundless source of life-giving nourishment.

Like a River Glorious

Like a river glorious, is God's perfect peace,
Over all victorious, in its bright increase;
Perfect, yet it floweth, fuller every day,
Perfect, yet it groweth, deeper all the way.

Refrain:
Stayed upon Jehovah, hearts are fully blest
Finding, as He promised, perfect peace and rest.

Hidden in the hollow of His blessed hand,
Never foe can follow, never traitor stand;
Not a surge of worry, not a shade of care,
Not a blast of hurry touch the spirit there.

Refrain

Every joy or trial falleth from above,
Traced upon our dial by the Sun of Love;
We may trust Him fully all for us to do.
They who trust Him wholly find Him wholly true.

Refrain

—Frances R. Havergal, 1876

Like a River Glorious

Lloyd Larson
Tune: WYE VALLEY
by James Mountain

Duration: 2:55

LT

pedal harmonically

Thoughts from Lloyd…

He Hideth My Soul

When I was a child growing up, my family of seven often did summer vacations in the family camper. This approach to family vacations had more to do with budgetary constraints than, let's say, noble aspirations like "family bonding." Regardless, I remember several occasions when a storm would arise and we would be herded into the "protective" environment of the camper. In retrospect, I realize there was really nothing overly protective about a fold-out camper with an exterior largely composed of canvas. But at the same time, I recall the sense of peace and protection which surrounded me in the form of family and love as we waited out each storm.

Whenever I hear this hymn, I am reminded of the fact that God never promises that life will be without its storms, for they come for all of us. However, as this text reminds us, we are assured that the Author of life provides us with a place of safety (a cleft in the rock) until the storm passes by. Some storms pass quickly, some take much longer, and some seem to have no end in sight. Regardless, we do not experience them alone. And some day, my faith tells me, I am assured of residence in a place where there will be no more pain, heartache or storms.

He Hideth My Soul

A wonderful Savior is Jesus my Lord,
A wonderful Savior to me;
He hideth my soul in the cleft of the rock,
Where rivers of pleasure I see.

Refrain:
He hideth my soul in the cleft of the rock
That shadows a dry, thirsty land;
He hideth my life with the depths of His love,
And covers me there with His hand,
And covers me there with His hand.

A wonderful Savior is Jesus my Lord,
He taketh my burden away;
He holdeth me up, and I shall not be moved,
He giveth me strength as my day.

Refrain

With numberless blessings each moment He crowns,
And filled with His fullness divine,
I sing in my rapture, oh, glory to God
For such a Redeemer as mine!

Refrain

When clothed in His brightness, transported I rise
To meet Him in clouds of the sky,
His perfect salvation, His wonderful love
I'll shout with the millions on high.

Refrain

—Fanny Crosby, 1890

He Hideth My Soul

Lloyd Larson
Tune: **KIRKPATRICK**
by William J. Kirkpatrick

Tenderly, freely ♩ = ca. 92

Duration: 3:30

Thoughts from Mary...

I Need Thee Every Hour

I have a special place in my heart for the old hymns. Not only do they represent our great heritage of faith, but the spirit of the words and music never seems to grow old. Just a few notes of an old gospel song cause me to reflect on persons and events that shape who I am today. As I sang and played through this great hymn, I was reminded of a Sunday evening sing-along many years ago when our music minister took requests from the congregation. Wanting to participate but not having a particular favorite, I raised my hand and requested a random page number. This was the hymn that was sung. When we got to the chorus, the instrumentalists, on cue from our minister, let the congregation sing unaccompanied. I thought it was the best singing of the night! Ever since that time, this hymn has touched my heart in a deeply personal way because, just as He was there for me as a child, I still claim these words: *Every hour, I need Thee.*

I Need Thee Every Hour

I need Thee every hour, most gracious Lord;
No tender voice like Thine can peace afford.

Refrain:
I need Thee, O I need Thee;
Every hour I need Thee;
O bless me now, my Savior,
I come to Thee.

I need Thee every hour, stay Thou nearby;
Temptations lose their power when Thou art nigh.

Refrain

I need Thee every hour, in joy or pain;
Come quickly and abide, or life is in vain.

Refrain

I need Thee every hour; teach me Thy will;
And Thy rich promises in me fulfill.

Refrain

I need Thee every hour, most Holy One;
O make me Thine indeed, Thou blessed Son.

Refrain

—Annie S. Hawks, 1872

I Need Thee Every Hour

Mary McDonald
Tune: **NEED**
by Robert Lowry, 1826-1899

Duration: 2:45

LT

18

Thoughts from Mary...

Tell It to Jesus

Serving as an editor for the Lorenz Corporation over the past sixteen years, I chose this hymn to honor the hymn's composer, Edmund S. Lorenz, founder of the Lorenz Publishing Company in 1890. It has long been a favorite gospel song of mine and was among the first I ever played in church. Once mastering all the notes composed by Mr. Lorenz, it was only natural to begin adding my own gospel style to really bring these words to life. This particular arrangement has a swing/jazz "feel," and was difficult to notate all the notes I was actually playing! I want you to have fun with the music and not worry too much about every detail. As I always say, if you hit it wrong, hit it strong! More importantly, let the spirit of the music inspire you to lead others just as this spirited tune by E. S. Lorenz has inspired me.

Tell It to Jesus

Are you weary, are you heavy hearted?
Tell it to Jesus, tell it to Jesus.
Are you grieving over joys departed?
Tell it to Jesus alone.

Refrain:
Tell it to Jesus, tell it to Jesus,
He is a Friend that's well known.
You've no other such a friend or brother,
Tell it to Jesus alone.

Do the tears flow down your cheeks unbidden?
Tell it to Jesus, tell it to Jesus.
Have you sins that to men's eyes are hidden?
Tell it to Jesus alone.

Refrain
Do you fear the gathering clouds of sorrow?
Tell it to Jesus, tell it to Jesus.

Are you anxious what shall be tomorrow?
Tell it to Jesus alone.

Refrain

Are you troubled at the thought of dying?
Tell it to Jesus, tell it to Jesus.
For Christ's coming kingdom are you sighing?
Tell it to Jesus alone.

Refrain

—*Edmund S. Lorenz, 1876;*
  tr. Jeremiah E. Rankin, 1880

Tell It to Jesus

Mary McDonald
Tune: DAYTON
by Edmund S. Lorenz, 1854-1942

Duration: 2:15

LT

24

70/1662L-24

Thoughts from Ruth...

I Know Whom I Have Believed

When I was little, the text to this song really spoke to me. I don't know why God chooses to love us, to save us, and I certainly don't claim to understand how it all works, but I do know that His salvation is sure and complete. It's truly a case of "It's all in Whom you know!"

I've always loved to set scripture to music, and I think that is another thing that appealed to me about this piece—the chorus is 2 Timothy 1:12, verbatim, with the verses giving the human questioning viewpoint, answered by the Biblical promise.

The lilting melody of this piece is so joyful, so light-hearted, it always brought joy to my heart when we sang it. I can imagine the hymn writers being really happy when they wrote this song—happy with the assurance that Jesus is all that we need, despite our limitations, our fears, and our doubts.

I Know Whom I Have Believed

I know not why God's wondrous grace
To me He hath made known,
Nor why, unworthy, Christ in love
Redeemed me for His own.

Refrain:
But I know Whom I have believed,
And am persuaded that He is able
To keep that which I've committed
Unto Him against that day.

I know not how this saving faith
To me He did impart,
Nor how believing in His Word
Wrought peace within my heart.

Refrain

I know not how the Spirit moves,
Convincing us of sin,
Revealing Jesus through the Word,
Creating faith in Him.

Refrain

I know not what of good or ill
May be reserved for me,
Of weary ways or golden days,
Before His face I see.

Refrain

I know not when my Lord may come,
At night or noonday fair,
Nor if I walk the vale with Him,
Or meet Him in the air.

Refrain

—*Daniel W. Whittle, 1883*

I Know Whom I Have Believed

Ruth Elaine Schram
Tune: **EL NATHAN**
by James McGranahan

Duration: 1:30

LT

Thoughts from Ruth...

Beneath the Cross of Jesus

This has always been a favorite hymn of mine. What a precious place to stand, under the shadow of my Savior!

As a child, sometimes the metaphors to hymn texts were lost on me, but I memorized those words and still sing them today—with much more understanding and appreciation not only for the poetry, but also the meaning behind it. I'm so thankful for the tremendous heritage of Christian music that is represented by this collection of gospel hymns.

Musically, I have always found this hymn to be ahead of its time—filled with interesting chords and accidentals that imply a deep understanding of music—not only theory but the practical implementation of it, coupled with a beautiful, memorable melody. The very things that, as a writer, I strive for with every piece of music I write!

Beneath the Cross of Jesus

Beneath the cross of Jesus I fain would take my stand,
The shadow of a mighty rock within a weary land;
A home within the wilderness, a rest upon the way,
From the burning of the noontide heat, and the burden of the day.

O safe and happy shelter, O refuge tried and sweet,
O trysting place where Heaven's love and Heaven's justice meet!
As to the holy patriarch that wondrous dream was given,
So seems my Savior's cross to me, a ladder up to heaven.

There lies beneath its shadow but on the further side
The darkness of an awful grave that gapes both deep and wide
And there between us stands the cross two arms outstretched to save
A watchman set to guard the way from that eternal grave.

Upon that cross of Jesus mine eye at times can see
The very dying form of One Who suffered there for me;
And from my stricken heart with tears two wonders I confess;
The wonders of redeeming love and my unworthiness.

I take, O cross, thy shadow for my abiding place;
I ask no other sunshine than the sunshine of His face;
Content to let the world go by to know no gain or loss,
My sinful self my only shame, my glory all the cross.

—*Elizabeth C. Clephane, 1868*

Beneath the Cross of Jesus

Ruth Elaine Schram
Tune: **ST. CHRISTOPHER**
by Frederick C. Maker

With freedom and fluid motion ♩. = 72

Duration: 2:25

www.lorenz.com

LT

32

70/1662L-32

Thoughts from Larry...

He Leadeth Me

I grew up one block away from Judson Baptist Church in Oak Park, Illinois, which made it very convenient for me to attend morning services, Sunday school, youth choir, Sunday night youth meetings, evening services, and various other activities throughout the week. Another side benefit was being able to hear the carillon that pealed forth from the steeple every weekday at noon. On my way home from grade school for lunch, the bells would play a selection of hymns that became very familiar to me over the years.

One that I remember distinctly was *He Leadeth Me*, which was written during the American Civil War by Joseph H. Gilmore and William B. Bradbury. The lyrics grew out of a sermon on the 23rd Psalm that Gilmore preached as a young pastor. Bradbury's melody moves over a wide range, but always returns serenely to the tonic; perhaps a picture of wandering sheep returning to their shepherd? For me, this hymn will always be tied to the sound of the bells, and I have incorporated that sound into this arrangement. I have dedicated this version to my pastor and his wife, Mark and Anita Bubeck, who ministered to me from junior high years into adulthood.

He Leadeth Me

He leadeth me, O blessed thought!
O words with heav'nly comfort fraught!
Whate'er I do, where'er I be
Still 'tis God's hand that leadeth me.

Refrain:
He leadeth me, He leadeth me,
By His own hand He leadeth me;
His faithful follower I would be,
For by His hand He leadeth me.

Sometimes 'mid scenes of deepest gloom,
Sometimes where Eden's bowers bloom,
By waters still, over troubled sea,
Still 'tis His hand that leadeth me.

Refrain

Lord, I would place my hand in Thine,
Nor ever murmur nor repine;
Content, whatever lot I see,
Since 'tis my God that leadeth me.

Refrain

And when my task on earth is done,
When by Thy grace the vict'ry's won,
E'en death's cold wave I will not flee,
Since God through Jordan leadeth me.

Refrain

—Joseph H. Gilmore, 1862

to Mark and Anita Bubeck

He Leadeth Me

Larry Shackley
Tune: HE LEADETH ME
by William B. Bradbury

Duration: 2:55

Thoughts from Larry...

Heavenly Sunlight

As a youth, my church had two distinct personalities: morning and evening. Morning services featured a robed choir, stately hymns, and classical organ music played on a pipe organ. Evening services were livelier, with piano added to the mix, tremolo added to the organ, and a lot more singing by the congregation. Our repertoire was chosen from the beloved gospel songs of the late 19th century, with names like Fanny Crosby, Ira D. Sankey, Philip P. Bliss, and Robert Lowry predominating.

One of my favorites was *Heavenly Sunlight*, written by George Harrison Cook in 1899. Cook was a lifetime church musician and preacher, whose one lasting contribution was this boisterous gospel hymn about the joys of walking with Christ. In our evening services at Judson Baptist, the song leader was Dick Jahns, who somehow balanced a career in banking with raising a family, singing in the choir, serving as a deacon, and teaching Sunday School classes for rowdy high-schoolers. This arrangement is dedicated to Dick and his wife, Sharon, with thanks for their influence and encouragement at an important time of my life.

Heavenly Sunlight

Walking in sunlight all of my journey;
Over the mountains, through the deep vale;
Jesus has said, "I'll never forsake thee,"
Promise divine that never can fail.

Refrain:
Heavenly sunlight, heavenly sunlight,
Flooding my soul with glory divine:
Hallelujah, I am rejoicing,
Singing His praises, Jesus is mine.

Shadows around me, shadows above me,
Never conceal my Savior and Guide;
He is the Light, in Him is no darkness;
Ever I'm walking close to His side.

Refrain

In the bright sunlight, ever rejoicing,
Pressing my way to mansions above;
Singing His praises gladly I'm walking,
Walking in sunlight, sunlight of love.

Refrain

—*Henry J. Zelley, 1899*

to Dick and Sharon Jahns

Heavenly Sunlight

Larry Shackley
Tune: **HEAVENLY SUNLIGHT**
by George H. Cook

Duration: 2:25

www.lorenz.com

40

Thoughts from Pepper...

The Solid Rock

After a two-day hike deep into the Grand Tetons of Wyoming, we camped at the bottom of a very steep trail leading up to Table Rock. I spent the evening looking at the formidable mountain, wondering if we would be able to make it to the top.

Much of the next morning's hike was spent inching our way up the steep, rocky path. With seventy-pound backpacks, we climbed the mountain, one step at a time, holding onto large rocks for support. Sometimes we would step on loose stones which would fall away beneath our feet, down the mountainside.

Between my slow, tentative steps, I found myself singing this hymn: *On Christ, the solid rock I stand* (step, pause for two breaths), *all other ground is sinking sand* (step, pause for a breath); *All other ground is sinking sand* (breath, breath).

As a young man, I didn't realize this was a perfect illustration of our faith in Christ. Certainly, life is sometimes a step-by-step uphill climb. Through it all, we must somehow remember to center on our faith in Christ.

In this arrangement, I wanted to communicate this upward journey with the inevitable struggles. Above the ascending, sometimes unexpected movement of the chords, there is the sure melody of *The Solid Rock*. As our lives take many unexpected turns, we seek to hold our faith sure as we stand firm on the Solid Rock.

The Solid Rock

My hope is built on nothing less
Than Jesus' blood and righteousness.
I dare not trust the sweetest frame,
But wholly trust in Jesus' Name.

Refrain:
On Christ the solid Rock I stand,
All other ground is sinking sand;
All other ground is sinking sand.

When darkness seems to hide His face,
I rest on His unchanging grace.
In every high and stormy gale,
My anchor holds within the veil.

Refrain

His oath, His covenant, His blood,
Support me in the whelming flood.
When all around my soul gives way,
He then is all my Hope and Stay.

Refrain

When He shall come with trumpet sound,
Oh may I then in Him be found.
Dressed in His righteousness alone,
Faultless to stand before the throne.

Refrain

—*Edward Mote, ca. 1834*

The Solid Rock
My Hope Is Built on Nothing Less

Pepper Choplin
Tune: **SOLID ROCK**
by William B. Bradbury

Duration: 3:00

LT

46

70/1662L-46

Thoughts from Pepper...

I've Got the Joy

It was always a treat to go to my grandmother's house and play with my cousins. On special occasions, we would spend the night and go to church with them at Piney Grove Baptist Church.

For the children's Sunday School assembly, my Aunt Nancy played the piano and led us in singing from a children's songbook. We would belt out favorites such as *O How I Love Jesus* and *Do, Lord*. (The big boys would add the extra part: *way beyond the blue—BLUE, BLUE, BLUE.*)

I've Got the Joy was one of those assembly songs. The first verse was catchy and was certainly easy to sing. However, I never quite got the second verse right—*I've got the peace that passeth understanding.* The King James version "passeth" would stick under my tongue and cause me to lisp the whole line.

But all in all, we got the message from these singing sessions. We learned that this faith thing was something to be happy about, something we could hold on to and share with others.

This arrangement was meant to convey simple UNADULTerated joy. The damper pedal should be saved for the slower section. I encourage you to play the fast passages with all the vitality and "jumpiness" of a fidgety children's Sunday School class.

As you play this with a bright sense of joy, perhaps it will serve as a musical smile to encourage you and your congregation in the faith.

I've Got the Joy

I've got the joy, joy, joy, joy
Down in my heart,
Down in my heart,
Down in my heart;
I've got the joy, joy, joy, joy
Down in my heart,
Down in my heart to stay.

I've got the peace that passeth understanding
Down in my heart,
Down in my heart,
Down in my heart;
I've got the peace that passeth understanding
Down in my heart,
Down in my heart to stay.

I've got the love of Jesus, love of Jesus
Down in my heart,
Down in my heart,
Down in my heart;
I've got the love of Jesus, love of Jesus
Down in my heart,
Down in my heart to stay.

For there is therefore now no condemnation
Down in my heart,
Down in my heart,
Down in my heart;
For there is therefore now no condemnation
Down in my heart,
Down in my heart to stay.

—*George W. Cooke*

I've Got the Joy

Pepper Choplin
Tune by George W. Cooke

Duration: 2:15

LT

Thoughts from Mark...

For the Beauty of the Earth

As I write these comments, it is cold outside and winter is in full force. However, I know that spring will indeed come, and with it delicate spring flowers and new buds on the trees will appear. No matter what the season, it's easy to see the beauty of the earth that God has created for us to enjoy. My arrangement of *For the Beauty of the Earth* reminds me of that first, fresh taste of spring. With a time signature in $\frac{5}{4}$, the melody floats along in a gently rhythmic fashion, much like a spring breeze. This favorite text from my youth is a wonderful reminder to be grateful for God's gift of nature.

For the Beauty of the Earth

For the beauty of the earth,
For the glory of the skies,
For the love which from our birth
Over and around us lies:

Refrain:
Lord of all, to Thee we raise
This our hymn of grateful praise.

For the wonder of each hour
Of the day and of the night,
Hill and vale, and tree and flow'r,
Sun and moon, and stars of light:

Refrain

For the joy of human love,
Brother, sister, parent, child,
Friends on earth, and friends above,
For all gentle thoughts and mild:

Refrain

For the church that evermore
Lifteth holy hands above,
Off'ring up on ev'ry shore
Her pure sacrifice of love:

Refrain

For the joy of ear and eye,
For the heart and mind's delight,
For the mystic harmony
Linking sense to sound and sight:

Refrain

For Thyself, best Gift Divine!
To our race so freely giv'n;
For that great, great love of Thine,
Peace on earth, and joy in heav'n:

Refrain

—Folliott S. Pierpoint, 1864

For the Beauty of the Earth

Mark Hayes
Tune: **DIX**
by Conrad Kocher

Duration: 1:20

www.lorenz.com LT

Thoughts from Mark...

Standing on the Promises

As a youth I grew up singing evangelical hymns and gospel songs in church. I especially liked the ones where the part-writing featured a separate bass line or countermelody that had different words and rhythms from the melody. *Standing on the Promises* was one of those songs. Singing something other than the melody was a good way to sight-read and kept me engaged in the music. My musical tastes have evolved since then, but my fondness for gospel music is still there. In this setting of *Standing on the Promises*, I've chosen a decidedly contemporary feel, featuring some jazz harmonies and rhythms. One performance tip I might suggest: keep the tempo steady and don't rush. When you play syncopations, it's crucial to keep the strong beats firm and true. Swing the sixteenth notes, not the eighths. Feel the slow, steady pulse of the song as you rest in the unshakeable promises of God.

Standing on the Promises

Standing on the promises of Christ my King,
Through eternal ages let His praises ring,
Glory in the highest, I will shout and sing,
Standing on the promises of God.

Refrain:
Standing, standing,
Standing on the promises of God my Savior;
Standing, standing,
I'm standing on the promises of God.

Standing on the promises that cannot fail,
When the howling storms of doubt and fear assail,
By the living Word of God I shall prevail,
Standing on the promises of God.

Refrain

Standing on the promises I now can see
Perfect, present cleansing in the blood for me;
Standing in the liberty where Christ makes free,
Standing on the promises of God.

Refrain

Standing on the promises of Christ the Lord,
Bound to Him eternally by love's strong cord,
Overcoming daily with the Spirit's sword,
Standing on the promises of God.

Refrain

Standing on the promises I cannot fall,
Listening every moment to the Spirit's call
Resting in my Savior as my all in all,
Standing on the promises of God.

Refrain

—R. Kelso Carter, 1886

Standing on the Promises

Mark Hayes
Tune: **PROMISES**
by R. Kelso Carter

Duration: 2:15

Also in the *Hymns We Love* series...

Hymns We Love

70/1573L

Level 2 · We asked several of the top composers for worship services today to pick two of their favorite hymns and create new settings to include in this compilation. Not surprisingly, the results were (and are) wonderful. Amazingly, there were no duplications of titles. All, however, are refreshingly unique and represent a diverse array of musical styles. We also asked each arranger to share why they chose a particular title and, perhaps, why a certain style was chosen for this setting. And viola!...we now offer you this collection of hymns expressly created by these composers as a wonderful addition for any church pianist's library.

Pepper Choplin – *Sweet By and By · Marching to Zion*

Mark Hayes – *Of the Father's Love Begotten · To God Be the Glory*

Lloyd Larson – *Crown Him with Many Crowns · Jesus Paid It All*

Mary McDonald – *Morning Has Broken · Come, Christians, Join to Sing*

Ruth Elaine Schram – *Love Lifted Me · Near to the Heart of God*

Larry Shackley – *Praise to the Lord, the Almighty · Day by Day*

Carols We Love

70/1622L

Level 2 · As a logical continuation of the series, we asked these talented composers for new settings of two of their favorite carols. As before, we also requested that the composers tell us why they picked their two carols and perhaps why they chose to set them in a particular style. Here, then, is the formidable result: *Carols We Love*, now ready to be an integral part of your Christmas repertoire for worship services or simply for personal enjoyment.

Mark Hayes – *God Rest You Merry, Gentlemen · Carol of the Bells*

Lloyd Larson – *Lo! How a Rose E'er Blooming · He Is Born, the Divine Christ Child*

Mary McDonald – *Away in a Manger · Angels We Have Heard on High*

Ruth Elaine Schram – *Silent Night · Angels, From the Realms of Glory*

Larry Shackley – *Sing We Now of Christmas · The Friendly Beasts*

Pepper Choplin – *O Little Town of Bethlehem · There's a Song in the Air*